Happy, happy birthday to
my friend Peg!
XO - Tnen 4.10.00

≈ For Your Garden ≈

HANGING BASKETS AND PLANTERS

For Your Garden

HANGING BASKETS AND PLANTERS

TERI DUNN

FRIEDMAN/FAIRFAX
PUBLISHERS

DEDICATION
To Shawn, Wes, and Tris, with all my love.
For Kathleen Kearns and her beautiful balcony plantings—and all the creative container
gardens around the village of Rockport that inspired me.

ACKNOWLEDGMENTS
Thanks, as always, to Susan Lauzau. Special thanks to Lola Stanton and Amanda Senten.

A FRIEDMAN/FAIRFAX BOOK

Library of Congress Cataloging-in-Publication Data available upon request.

ISBN 1-56799-955-7

Editors: Hallie Einhorn and Susan Lauzau
Art Director: Jeff Batzli
Designer: Jennifer Markson
Photography Editor: Erin Feller
Production Managers: Ingrid McNamara and Leslie Wong

Color separations by Fine Arts Repro House Co., Ltd.
Printed in Hong Kong by Midas Printing, Ltd.

1 3 5 7 9 10 8 6 4 2

For bulk purchases and special sales, please contact:
Friedman/Fairfax Publishers
Attention: Sales Department
15 West 26th Street
New York, NY 10010
212/685-6610 FAX 212/685-1307

Visit our website:
www.metrobooks.com

Contents

INTRODUCTION

*P*ossessing the wondrous ability to introduce garden touches practically anywhere, including high overhead, hanging baskets and planters open up a world of possibilities. Some plant lovers rely upon these features to extend their gardens to "untillable" areas. Others rely upon them because of space and time constraints. After all, these miniature gardens are less labor-intensive than, say, caring for a major perennial border. But they can be just as beautiful to behold and as satisfying to nurture. They also have the advantage of being more intimate—easier to see, touch, sniff, and appreciate daily.

This book is meant to jog your creativity. You will see lovely and unique plant choices, as well as exciting pairings of flowers and foliage. And the planters themselves come in all sorts of materials, shapes, sizes, and styles. Whether you prefer wood or stone, large or small, formal or casual, handcrafted or machine-made, the containers that best suit your needs are out there. Many even boast supporting hardware that is attractive in its own right. You might want to choose a planter that can be deftly integrated with such architectural features as a window, wall, or porch. Or you may simply opt for a scene-stealer—a container so original and stunning that it stops visitors in their tracks.

Whatever you do, have fun. Designing and putting out planters is like the theater. You can let the container be the star or have the plants within take center stage. You can replant or reposition. You can direct attention to highlights (or deflect attention from flaws) in your garden area. You can delight, surprise, and entertain.

With regard to caring for these diminutive gardens, make sure that there are drainage holes, and water often, especially in warm weather. Fertilize regularly because the plants will quickly deplete whatever nutrients were originally in the soil mix. If the plants get lanky, cut them back and wait for a fresh flush of growth. If leaves or flowers are sparse, and you are otherwise providing good care, chances are the planter is in need of a sunnier spot. In the end, you will agree that tending to these small gardens is easy and highly gratifying.

OPPOSITE: What makes this balcony so irresistible is the color scheme. The gardener has chosen plenty of different plants and pots, and varied means of displaying them, but has stuck to a unifying theme of yellow and red.

ABOVE: A wall pot basically looks like half of a regular container, with a flat surface to go flush against the wall. Obtain the anchoring hardware from the same supplier, and hook the configuration to the wall prior to planting, just to make sure it holds. Then remove the setup, and fill it with lightweight potting mix and a few plants. As they begin to grow, the plants will hide the supports from view and make for a pretty picture. The gardener here has selected a pot with a painted-on flower that resembles the blooms planted within.

ABOVE: The principles often used in putting bouquets together can also be applied to window boxes. Observe how the bright orange and yellow nasturtiums sit in the center, flanked by modest red, pink, and white flowers. To round off the arrangement, the sides are gathered together by sprays of small purple lobelia blooms. The result is balanced, interesting, and attractive.

ABOVE: A window with green trim will flatter any color of flower. Here, a white curtain inside offers a clean backdrop, its delicate fabric echoing the softness of the petals. Matching tones are provided by the broad geranium foliage and the flowing white lobelia. The pinks and purples, though, immediately grab the eye.

ABOVE: This beauty is so laden with blooms that the basket is completely hidden from view. But it was not so at the outset; the gardener has surely encouraged the prolific show by keeping all the plants well watered and coaxing them along with regular doses of fertilizer. All in all, this is really not much effort to expend for such a fabulous display. And if your space is limited, just one basket like this can be your pride and joy.

ABOVE: Yellow oncidium orchids flash like sunbeams from shadowy tree branches. The plain, wood-slat container is practical because orchid roots need excellent drainage and ventilation, but the receptacle also acts as an understated supporter, deftly blending in with the bark of the tree. All attention is directed where it should be—to the radiant tiers of yellow.

ABOVE: Gardeners weary of winter and eager for spring start their containers early. Here, such favorites as 'Tête-à-tête' daffodils and snowdrops burst into bloom above a complementary mound of variegated ivy. The iron hanger and metal chain provide the support needed for the rather bulky basket.

ABOVE: Small pots can be attached to fences or trellises with sturdy clips, available at some garden centers and in various specialty nursery catalogs. Here, such clip and pot combinations are full of bright primulas, which should keep blooming for many weeks, especially in cool, early spring weather. The wall behind the cheery display has been treated with a green finish to provide a subtle, natural-looking backdrop.

RIGHT: A porch gains privacy with the help of fully packed planters. In fact, the barrier is now nearly twice as high, thanks to the purple petunias and delicate white blooms. While most of the sitting area is shielded from prying eyes, people relaxing on the porch are still able to take in the surrounding scenery.

ABOVE: A recessed window benefits greatly from a heavily planted box. In such a situation, the flowers should be bright enough to burst forth from the shadows. And, as in the landscaping of shade areas in the garden proper, plants with variegated leaves, such as these ivies, work particularly well. Note how the texture of these leaves echoes that of the stone surface.

ABOVE: Do you have a wall that is cloaked in green ivy? Before the window gets lost to view, put in a window box and fill it with billowing, bold-colored flowers, such as these red petunias. Red geraniums or begonias, or any other candidate with large flowers, would also do the trick.

ABOVE: A low stone wall with a broad, flat top can be an ideal place upon which to rest a container. Just make sure that the vessel is heavy and sturdy enough to stay where you set it. No wind or summer storm is likely to dislodge this massive stone urn. You should also plant enough in the container to achieve a show on all sides, for the ensemble will surely be an attention-getter for anyone coming or going. In this somewhat shady spot, the gardener has wisely used plenty of shade-loving tuberous begonia plants, accented with trailing ivy.

RIGHT: A balcony in the sun is a perfect spot to grow herbs. Here, basil and parsley (both curly-leaved and flat-leaved) thrive in a decorative planter. The container is small enough to hang comfortably on the railing, but large enough to support the herbs' growth. Creating a powerful sense of harmony, the designs on the planter echo the pattern on the railing.

RIGHT: The edge of a porch abounds with excitement, thanks to a planter filled with boisterous, somewhat unorthodox plant choices. Opening their faces up to the sun, eager 'Plaisir' tulips can't help but bring a smile to those they encounter. These flowers' bare stems are hidden by horned violets (*Viola cornuta*) and tufts of *Saxifraga × arendsii*, which weave smoothly in between to tie everything together. Bulbs are easy to grow in a container as long as they are buried several inches below the soil mix's surface. Reminiscent of a picket fence, the blue planter sets a traditional tone.

ABOVE: Broad, shallow steps and a low wall practically beg for the adornment of containerized plants. Using clay pots to match the bricks is a nice touch, and repeating the same flowers, or at least the same colors, from one pot to the next supplies a unified feel.

ABOVE: Do you have a lot of space to cover? Think big and think repetition. A progression of large pots is certainly up to the job. Since such vessels offer room for plenty of soil, generous plantings are possible.

Chapter One

HANGING BASKETS

A hanging basket that displays a little extra creativity can revitalize part of your home's exterior or a corner of your yard. Indeed, it can make all the difference in the world. Where once was a lackluster spot, now hangs something unexpectedly beautiful.

So seize the opportunity. Don't settle for a pedestrian green plastic basket, preplanted, purchased haphazardly at a local market—a basket that you bring home only to find doesn't fit in with your landscape. Instead, choose the location first and prepare the container second. Is the spot you have in mind shady for most of the day? If so, find out which plants prosper in shade; vivid tuberous begonias are a splendid choice, as are imaginative combinations of various foliage plants or fragrant herbs. Perhaps your targeted site is a small nook that is barren of color. Then compose something cheerful and vivacious to bring the area to life.

If you don't expect the plants to cover the container, choose a basket that's decorative. There are many different kinds of hanging baskets, as well as pots that can be rigged to hangers. Plastic containers are light and practical, and a little hunting can turn up a rainbow of color choices. Other options run the gamut from wire baskets, lined with sphagnum moss, to unique handcrafted ceramic containers.

Remember that a pot full of soil mix and plants, watered, can be heavy. This will be a factor not only on the first day as you endeavor to hang your creation, but also in the weeks to come. The pot must be sturdy, and the supports appropriately strong. The overhead hook or hanger must also be up to the job.

One last practical note: give some thought to how high or low you want the basket to hang. Too high, and not only will it be difficult to care for, but few people will be able to admire it properly. Too low, and you run the risk of creating an obstacle rather than a lovely decoration!

ABOVE: There's something thrilling about this small basket of ordinary geraniums. Poised daintily overhead, it exudes an air of simple elegance. The design of the wooden container echoes the lines of the house, while the scarlet flowers burst onto the scene to supply rich color.

OPPOSITE: The theme of pink, with its many variations, has been used to create a memorable feast for the eyes. Tutulike blossoms of fuchsia and some bright geraniums steal the spotlight, but a supporting cast of soft-hued lobelia and shell-pink petunias graciously provides backup.

ABOVE LEFT: Common plants—lobelia, petunias, begonias, daisylike bidens—are made uncommon when combined artfully in a hanging planter. This gardener chose primary colors to make the displays as clean and bold as possible against the pale hues of the house.

ABOVE RIGHT: Petunias used to be bedding plants only, and they were so frequently employed that most people became blind to their charms. Then, not too long ago, breeders developed petunias with trailing habits (and somewhat smaller flowers). These have turned out to be terrific hanging basket candidates, thanks to their compactness and propensity to bloom like gangbusters. They are also fairly drought-tolerant, so they can weather some neglect and still look great. Shown here is 'Hot Pink'; another favorite is 'Purple Wave'.

OPPOSITE: With its soft green hues and lush nature, *Helichrysum petiolare* appears to be a favorite of the gardener residing here, for it has been planted in the ground, as well as in the overhead baskets. This echo effect is a good plan if you garden in a limited amount of space and want to create the illusion of bounty.

ABOVE: Imagine how static this scene would be without the pair of hanging baskets, whose bold red and white flowers inject welcome exuberance. By placing one basket over each bench, the gardener maintains the symmetrical composition of the hardscape, allowing the plants to live in harmony with the setting. The whiteness of the hangers is a finishing touch that ties all the elements together. Notice how the baskets are hung high enough overhead that they won't interfere with someone sitting below.

ABOVE: The close quarters of baskets have their advantages. As blooms spill over each other and weave into each other's "territories," color combinations become compressed and intimate. Thus, you won't be left wishing that the purple centers of the trailing petunias would call out the purple of the lobelia—they will.

ABOVE: Here's a basket with an innovative theme: colorful leaves. This artful mix includes ivy, its leaves splashed with cream, and *Carex* 'Evergold', a yellow, grassy sedge, which is fronted here by the variegated form of *Hakonechloa macra*. Red-leaved *Tellima* and yellow-flowered *Epimedium* also chime in, while pink-spiked heather (*Calluna* 'Silver Knight') sprays out behind. All of these are durable plants that keep their color for a long period of time, well into autumn. Clearly, a fair amount of effort went into assembling and planting this exciting basket, but the gardener is rewarded with easy maintenance and splendor.

ABOVE LEFT: Who says hanging baskets belong only on the porch? Here, suspended from a sturdy tree branch, a great show of pink trailing verbena infuses the surroundings with radiance. These flowers can go outdoors once temperatures begin to rise in early summer, by which time the tree blossoms will have passed and the new addition of color will be much appreciated.

ABOVE RIGHT: Clematis in a basket? We usually think of these big-flowered beauties as rangy vines that are ideal for mounting trellises. But this clematis, 'Silver Moon', works well here, as it is one of a handful of cultivars with an especially compact habit.

OPPOSITE: Moss-lined baskets not only add a natural-looking touch to your garden, but also provide excellent drainage for the plants grown within them. The moss acts as a reservoir, soaking up extra water and releasing it back into the soil mix as required. A little evaporation also takes place, increasing the local humidity. Such conditions are bliss for almost any plant, save succulents. Here, an arresting display is achieved as the flowers make their way through the openings of an intricate sphere.

LEFT: The rules change when it comes to container gardening. Creeping Jenny (*Lysimachia nummularia*) is such a rampant grower that most gardeners view it as a pest; however, in a hanging basket, it eagerly provides lush tresses of yellow blooms that you can count on. Similarly, red valerian (*Centranthus ruber*) is considered troublesome, as it often self-sows into spots where it is not wanted. Confined, though, it pumps out a continual supply of beautiful reddish flowers.

ABOVE: Lobelia—in blue, purple, or even pink or white—is a favorite edging plant, valued for its prolific flowering and agreeable nature. The trailing varieties are ideal for basket life, as they will quickly cascade over the side of a pot for a sumptuous and dependable display. Here, they adorn a cabin entrance and enhance the home's natural look.

LEFT: A traditional hanging ivy basket has been enhanced by the imaginative addition of amiable companions. A mound of ajuga, with its mottled leaves, adds a splash of color, while dense-growing lavender cotton (*Santolina chamaecyparissus*) contributes texture. The whole ensemble dresses up the white porch and brings those relaxing there one step closer to nature.

RIGHT: At the other end of the same porch, a basket of blooms hangs overhead, which just goes to show that containers lined up in a row don't have to sport the same plants for a harmonious effect. The symmetry of the scene is maintained by the placement of each basket beside a chair, while welcome variety is provided by the different colors and textures.

ABOVE LEFT: It is hard to say where the flowers planted in the ground end and the ones tumbling down from the suspended baskets begin. If a riot of color is your wish, this approach is definitely worth imitating. Just be sure to hang the baskets far enough out from the wall that you'll still be able to reach them for grooming and watering.

ABOVE RIGHT: The most striking hanging basket in this picture is the one at the top with the surprising plants—tomatoes and parsley. The tomato planted here is the cultivar 'Tumbler', which sports a naturally trailing habit. The parsley, a curly-leaved type, is a mound-former. Together, they charm the eye and entice the palate.

OPPOSITE: Solid brick and straight lines are immediately softened by a few hanging baskets. Note how the plants have been allowed to go a bit wild, billowing out over the confines of their pots. Together, they turn a staid setting into an inviting one.

Chapter Two

WINDOW BOXES

They may be small in size, but window boxes can certainly have a big impact. Their very presence transforms otherwise unused, uninteresting spots into gardens. Suddenly, there's life and color. Passersby will smile and pause to admire. Butterflies and hummingbirds might pay a visit if the plants you've chosen offer the nectar they love. Even people inside the house will enjoy glimpses of the display.

For some, such as apartment dwellers and other people with limited space or time, window boxes may provide the only opportunity to garden. Fortunately, window boxes can be fabulous showpieces, and the plants they contain can present a jaunty, even heroic bid for beauty. And you don't even have to use an actual window box. An array of pots on a sill can create quite the stir.

Although many think of window boxes as simply garden accents, attention to the plants and containers is still important—and rewarding. Perhaps you will want to create a color union between the flowers, the planter, and the outdoor furniture below. Or perhaps the paint treatment or architectural style of the window frame, sill, or shutters will provide the opportunity to create what is essentially a little vignette.

In any event, assure the success of your window box by making sure it is securely mounted so it can bear the weight of the contents. Provisions for water drainage are also key, so roots won't be subject to rot. Speaking of water, don't forget regular applications; window boxes tend to dry out surprisingly quickly. You may be able to reach the display from inside the house with a long-necked watering can, or from outside with a hose or watering wand.

A garden on this scale is easy to nurture and can be both cozy and lovely. And remember, the window that opens to flowers is truly a joyous place.

OPPOSITE: Geraniums are unique in that they come in a number of different forms, which you may combine if you so desire. Close inspection of this window box reveals that those in the center are regular bedding-plant geraniums, while the ones skirting the perimeter are ivy geraniums.

RIGHT: Painted walls and a colorful blue shutter issued a challenge for window gardening here. The dilemma was whether to include plants that matched the blue, the yellow, or the pink—or a combination. The decision to go with pink, the hue gracing the areas closest to and farthest away from the window, has caused the whole wall to be included in the viewer's impression. Thus, a tiny garden seems somehow larger.

LEFT: Spring is greeted in style with this sprightly window box, filled to the brim with pristine, white blooms. The monochromatic theme is jazzed up by the use of a variety of flowers, all of which contribute different looks and textures to the mix. Creamy daffodils tower above fragrant hyacinths, while spotless primulas and white-bordered ivy rest at their feet. In cool weather, this display will continue to look handsome for up to two weeks. When warmer weather arrives, everything except, perhaps, the ivy may be removed to make way for another seasonal show.

ABOVE: Bright white paint and a dark window are joined by pansies that mimic the effect; the flowers' interiors are dark and their edges white. Demure, unremarkable pots graciously house the flowers, but in no way detract from their shining performance.

OPPOSITE: Sitting pretty in the window, pink and red geraniums jump out against the pale beige and tan hues of the home's exterior. To keep the setting as colorful as possible, the gardener has set pots with more geraniums and some perky yellow and orange marigolds along the ground below. Carved architectural details on either side of the window cleverly extend the floral theme.

RIGHT: Cast-iron grates, often mounted over city windows for security reasons, are not easy to work with. A bold shout of color, as provided by these big-blossomed geraniums, is an inspiring choice. No longer is this window forbidding; indeed, it now looks like a handsome framed picture. The rectangular band of detailing at the bottom of the grate creates the illusion of a window box, even though the flowers really reside in a clay pot.

LEFT: You don't have to decorate a windowsill with colorful flowers. These elfish topiaries, in their handsome terra-cotta pots, form a bewitching vignette without help from any blooms. The symmetry of the composition and the way in which the plants are framed by the architectural trim establish a serene sense of order, but the jauntiness of the clipped plants exudes charm.

ABOVE: The exterior of a traditional-style building is greatly enhanced by a formal window box exhibit. Rising from a carpet of ivy and prostrate juniper is a diminutive, smiling urn planted with a fountain of slender-leaved sedge (*Carex* 'Sunshine'). In attendance are some compact-growing heaths (*Erica gracilis*) and coralbells (*Heuchera* 'Rachel'). Adding another type of container to a window box is an innovative idea, worthy of imitation if you can work the container into your composition so that it is neither too prominent nor overwhelmed.

ABOVE: Primary colors arise from a thickly planted window box on a narrow sill. All are harbingers of spring: tulips, grape hyacinths, primroses, and violas. To keep such an array looking its triumphant best for at least several weeks, fertilize every time you water (mix the plant food at half strength with the water) and pinch off any petal, flower, or leaf that isn't holding up to the rest of the show.

OPPOSITE: Herbs crowd a terra-cotta planter, shown off to good advantage by a comely lace curtain. From left are lavender, rosemary, sage, basil, parsley, and fennel, with a few flowers brought in for color. Herbs like to grow in clay containers; while they do need water to prosper, they don't care for soggy soil, and porous clay naturally wicks away excess moisture.

ABOVE: If you are lucky enough to inherit or find a window tray support that is this attractive, don't obscure it by plunking a window box on top of it. A few simple pots will highlight the charms of this prized feature. Here, pots made of terra-cotta stand out solidly against the white architectural trim and gauzy curtains while picking up the tones of the brick wall. To match the elegance of the support's swirling vine design, the gardener has chosen a group of formal-looking plants for the setting. The middle plant is a dwarf flowering hydrangea, which is flanked by small pieris plants.

OPPOSITE: Any gardener who willingly plants yellow loosestrife (*Lysimachia punctata*) knows he'll have blooms in abundance. So a profuse window box in the area is appropriate to complete the impression of bounty—and wildness. This planter has been given over entirely to a purple-flowered oxalis. The whole arrangement keeps the eye engaged at all levels.

Chapter Three

PLANTERS FOR WALLS AND FENCES

The wish to decorate every available nook, cranny, corner, railing, and surface of an area with plants is a passion. It is also a lot of fun. And there are many creative ways of filling these spaces with the foliage and blooms that you love.

Granted, walls and fences are frequently the bare spots of any garden, valued more for their utility than for their aesthetics. They define boundaries, enclose your sanctuary, and provide privacy. But there's no reason you can't also use them to add an extra measure of color and beauty.

Since walls and fences obviously cannot provide soil on their own, you must adorn them with pots or baskets of some sort. There are numerous clever ways to attach planters to the targeted surface. The necessary hangers and screws can be purchased wherever a wide selection of containers is available. And if all else fails, or if you simply prefer, you can just scoot a pot or two up close to the structure.

One advantage containers have on these vertical tableaus is that they are removable, and hence portable. Obviously, you could fill the same empty area with a flowering vine, an espaliered fruit tree, or a crush of flowers. But what if the plant doesn't prosper in that location? What if it looks plain or downright unappealing when it is not blooming or fruiting? Or what if your selection is simply slow to fill in its assigned space? With containerized plants, all you have to do is simply shift around the ones that aren't living up to their potential. Plus, you can change the contents of the containers as your whims and the seasons dictate. In the end, you'll get a display that you can rely on—right where you want it.

OPPOSITE: A vast brick wall is certainly monotonous to the eye, but what are your options? This gardener brought color to the scene by erecting a large trellis. Such a frame must be both strong enough and deep enough to hold all the flowerpots. It also needs to be attached securely to the wall so that the accumulated weight doesn't topple it.

RIGHT: An airy wrought-iron shelf is warmed by the addition of pelargonium ivy and purple flowers. If you include candles in the mix, make sure that the plants are far enough away from the flames that no leaves—either on the plants or falling off them—will catch on fire

ABOVE LEFT: A small portion of a wall is transformed into a garden microcosm, thanks to a compact array of potted plants and a soothing fountain.

ABOVE RIGHT: Imagine this scene without the eye-catching pot of flowers. The leafy plants—hosta below the wall and euonymus above—would seem to recede into the shadows. The soft pastel hues of the blossoms are an inspired choice because they not only brighten the corner but also provide refreshing contrast against the heavy-looking brick wall.

OPPOSITE: Resting on a brick ledge with an imposing wall in the background, bleeding hearts (*Dicentra spectabilis*) are a welcome sight. The weathered lead trough not only enhances the garden's charm but also echoes the texture of the wall.

ABOVE: Wall sconce containers are swiftly gaining popularity. Fashioned to be attached to walls or fences, they make endearing planters. Heat-tolerant plants, such as this pink verbena 'Aphrodite' and the accompanying herbs, thrive in these setups because walls capture and reflect warmth.

RIGHT: Slim wall-mounted containers bearing marigolds enhance the quaint look of this country dwelling. The wrap-around design of the attaching hardware creates the impression that the plants are being lovingly embraced. Plus, the fluid curves echo the rounded shapes of the leaves and flowers.

OPPOSITE: The vine may blanket the wall well, but it is not in bloom for long. Thus, the gardener has wedged in a number of pots on a narrow ledge to pick up the slack. They're filled with such long-blooming, easygoing annuals as alyssum, pansies, and petunias—plants that can be counted on to keep the spot colorful. If you have a similar situation in your yard but lack the helpful ledge, try tucking in a few tall, slender plant stands or supports.

RIGHT: Myriad flowers spring forth joyously from every inch of a narrow walled-in garden bed. This lush abundance was achieved with the help of hanging baskets displayed all along the wall.

ABOVE: For added pattern, try affixing pots to a trellis. Here, a once barren passage has been transformed into a verdant little garden. The stronger the trellis is, the more potted plants it will be able to exhibit.

RIGHT: A staggered arrangement of terra-cotta pots filled with marigolds and pansies enlivens a garden wall. The decision to use terra-cotta, which blends in with the naturalistic wattle background, allows the flowers to be the main focus of attention. The purple and gold color scheme is continued in the plantings below, creating a unified look.

LEFT: Visitors are warmly greeted at this doorway by a simple but utterly endearing basket stuffed with pansies. Better than a bouquet, the display of these durable little flowers lasts for months. The shape of the basket is reminiscent of a cornucopia, suggesting abundance.

ABOVE: A dim, uninteresting junction in a plain stone wall is made more intimate in scale and much more attractive with the addition of this planter. The white of the planter itself and the distinctive white cyclamen within dramatically brighten the scene; the variegated ivy also helps.

LEFT: There's something so spontaneous and playful about this old tin pail, casually hooked over a fence post and stuffed with flowering plants. It's as if the gardener scooped up the discarded pail and filled it on the run, temporarily placing it in a sunny spot. If your garage or basement doesn't yield any such containers, try a yard sale; there is much satisfaction and pleasure to be gained from rescuing such a castaway and giving it new life in your garden.

LEFT: If there's a wall or railing outside your kitchen, try growing some flowers in retired old pots and pans for a culinary theme. Since these cooking tools don't have drainage holes, the flowers will be better off if you plant them in a plastic pot that does, and then set them inside the pan. Surplus water can then be poured off easily.

RIGHT: Well-worn shoes nailed to the side of an entrance and filled with soil and plants create a whimsical and humorous diversion. With the shoes pointed downward and the plants growing up toward the sky, a riveting tug-of-war effect is achieved. Of course, part of the fun is encountering something on a vertical surface that we expect to see on a horizontal one.

Chapter Four

CONTAINERS FOR DECKS AND BALCONIES

If your gardening area is a deck, balcony, porch, or patio, don't feel deprived. There are more opportunities than you might realize for growing and displaying plants in such spaces. Innovative hangers, attractive containers, and all sorts of plants can enhance these settings.

Think about what you want. If a sense of complete enclosure is what you're looking for, then cram in as many pots as you can, and let their plants spill out and over and into one another. Maybe you'd prefer just enough decoration to obscure straight lines or dull surfaces. To achieve this effect, begin conservatively, setting out just a few planters or pots at first and adding more only if necessary.

If you are fortunate enough to have a deck or balcony with a great view, choose garden elements that don't clamor for attention—perhaps a few undecorated clay, plastic, or wooden containers filled with plants known for their handsome foliage. Don't forget that potted plants allow you to move, add, and delete with impunity, so you can always alter your display until it satisfies you.

While making the most of limited space is challenging, it is also rewarding. When flowers and trailing foliage dress up a confined spot, you will enjoy retreating there. Just be sure to leave a place to sit and savor the fruits of your efforts.

OPPOSITE: Hardly any space, hardly any light, yet look at what the gardener has accomplished. A variety of textured surfaces captures interest and makes the tiny area seem larger. A sculpted head, made of terra-cotta like the pots, adds a stylish aura of antiquity.

RIGHT: Planters that blend with the deck's surface, as well as with each other, can set the stage for a quietly beautiful display. When you have troughs and pillars as attractive as these, you'll want to prevent the plants from overtaking them—so keep those clippers handy.

ABOVE: One large, dramatic pot can set the mood in a confined area. If you are able to select plants that mesh with the colors on the container—as these variegated-leaved geraniums do (plain old geranium leaves would never have the same effect)—the resulting combination will stimulate the senses.

ABOVE: The lushness of this area is achieved through a common trick—but it works. Fill a number of pots, then arrange them in a stepped manner so that you create the sensation of great height in a limited amount of space (use shelves, chairs, cinder blocks, or even an old stepladder). Grow compatible plants—here, primarily orchids and ferns have been used—to establish harmony.

ABOVE: When you don't have much gardening space, devote your efforts to a full, varied pot display and lavish it with water and fertilizer. The edge of a deck is a wonderful spot for showing off such a labor of love.

ABOVE: Classic architecture is spiced up with a refreshing sense of spontaneity provided by an informal planter on a porch railing. Framed perfectly by the window, the planter projects the illusion that it is actually a window box. The lively and airy array of flowers seems to spill out a genuine welcome to all who pass.

ABOVE: To take advantage of every precious inch, a gardener has placed pots at all different levels on this balcony. A few folk-art decorations, namely the duck, rooster, and birdhouse, pop up throughout the display, heightening the charm of the busy garden.

ABOVE: Even under a light dusting of snow, pots can do much to dress up or disguise a low railing. However, if your winters are quite cold and snowy, it's better to empty the pots and bring them inside. Otherwise, freeze-and-thaw cycles may cause the terra-cotta to crack—not to mention the fact that the plants' roots will freeze. These small evergreens (among them a dwarf fir and a miniature spruce) are pretty tough, though.

ABOVE: Containers have made possible this gardener's dream of a bountiful, verdant sanctuary. By placing grasses and trees in planters, the gardener has allowed the surrounding greenery to advance onto the patio.

ABOVE: Owners of wooden decks frequently employ wooden planters. Thus, the use of metal containers serves up a refreshing surprise. The neutral silvery shine and clean smoothness mesh easily with the surroundings while at the same time drawing attention to the sprays of ornamental grasses within.

ABOVE: Bouquets are always welcome on tables indoors, but when you have outdoor tables, go for living, blooming plants, such as these vibrant crocuses. Even a small table on a balcony can support such a display. And in many instances, calling upon the service of a decorative table, such as this tiled one, yields more impressive results than using a traditional plant stand.

LEFT: When space is at a premium, creativity is in order. How about decorating a garden bench with potted plants? Since the seat was most likely made to support a fair amount of weight, you can feel free to load it up. Here, large tubs of hyacinths mingle with terra-cotta pots of daffodils. As spring turns to summer, you can discard these plants and replace them with new bloomers.

ABOVE: All the care that went into choosing containers and pots has paid off in this tiny spot at the edge of a patio. Spiky grape hyacinths (*Muscari*) and chubby yellow ranunculuses flourish in pots at ground level, while a terra-cotta cherub serves up a generous arrangement of tulips, pansies, and more ranunculuses, bringing these flowers to new heights.

ABOVE: A daring idea, but it works. A large pot full of arching flowers, most notably pink-and-white bleeding hearts (*Dicentra spectabilis*), sits prominently atop a pedestal, enhancing the view from the porch. If you try this, make sure that the stand or table is out of the way of direct traffic, so that it won't be toppled accidentally. A corner of a balcony or patio would be an ideal spot.

RIGHT: Deck gardens benefit greatly from at least one spectacular potted display. Choose a large pot, and pack it with exuberant growers. The favored formula is to situate one or two tall plants, preferably with spiky flowers or sprays of leaves, in the center and surround them with flowers that trail gently over the sides.

Photography Credits

A-Z Botanical Collection Ltd.:
pp. 21, 44, 58 bottom

©**R. Todd Davis**: pp. 11 left, 26 left,
46, 62 right

The Garden Picture Library: pp. 6,
12 left, 17 top, 17 bottom, 20, 30,
31, 36, 41, 42, 43, 54 left, 60, 65 left,
65 right, 68–69, 69 right, 70 left,
70 right

©**John Glover**: pp. 2, 10, 11 right,
22 left, 22 right, 23, 25 left, 25 right,
26 right, 28, 32 left, 32 right, 47, 48
left, 50, 53

House & Interiors: pp. 7, 14

©**Dency Kane**: pp. 27, 58 top

©**Marianne Majerus**: pp. 15, 35, 38,
40, 44, 54–55, 56, 57, 67

©**Charles Mann**: pp. 8, 9, 16, 18, 19,
24, 29, 49, 52, 62 left (designer:
Keeyla Meadows), 63, 66 (designer:
Bob Clark), 71

©**Clive Nichols**: pp.33 (designer:
Joan Murdy), 34, 37 (designer:
Anthony Noel), 48 right (designer:
Emma Lush), 51 (designer: Fiona
Lawrenson), 61 (designer: Emma
Lush)

©**Nance S. Trueworthy**: pp. 12–13,
39, 59, 64